IMAGINE WE TRADE BODIES WITH SHEEP

DUKE AL

LUCENT DREAMING

First edition

Imagine we Trade Bodies with Sheep
Published by Lucent Dreaming Ltd.
103 Bute Street, Cardiff, CF10 5AD

This book is set in a surreal, fictional universe.
All characters, incidents, and events are fictitious. Any resemblance to
real persons, living or dead, is purely coincidental.

Cover illustration © 2025 Dom Tsoi
Front cover and spine designed by Ry Foat.

ISBN 978-1-7396609-7-0

Lucent Dreaming acknowledges the financial support of
Books Council of Wales and Creative Wales.

CYNGOR LLYFRAU CYMRU
BOOKS COUNCIL of WALES

Mum

You are my rock.
I love you.

Content Warning:

This collection contains themes that some readers may find sensitive or distressing. Reader discretion is advised.

CONTENTS

Note from the Author

Growing up, I suffered deeply with intrusive thoughts. I still do. They attacked every second I was awake, eventually spilling into my dreams. These intrusive thoughts targeted my morals, ethics, values, things and people that I love. I fought every second, every minute of every day, to prove to myself that I wasn't a bad person. I felt guilt, I was shaken by shame, I performed debilitating, endless compulsions to try and neutralise my intrusive thoughts. I tried to prevent each irrational thought that had a hold on me from becoming a reality. I have Obsessive Compulsive Disorder (OCD). Feeling alone, I decided to write about these thoughts, how I was feeling; my brain told my hand, my hand told the pen, and the pen told the page. I escaped for a moment. Being diagnosed with Type 1 Diabetes, aged 23, the pen was there to help me articulate a rollercoaster of emotions. I learned and understood what my suffering meant. I had to go through the hardship to get to where I am now, to relate to those who are going through similar struggles.

I've always felt a passion, an urge to write about how I feel. To shine light upon the hatred that can often consume our society, in all of its tragedy, injustice and corruption.

I wanted to write about this as if we had the bodies of sheep, to show how ridiculous, absurd and cruel humanity can be. Morals, ethics and values seem to be drifting away from society. Selfishness is leading the way. However, it was important for me to sprinkle the good and the love that humanity, by nature, still has. A little bit of good and a little bit of love go a long way, showing how powerful and needed they both are.

Are you ready to remove the wool from your eyes?

IMAGINE WE TRADE BODIES WITH SHEEP

Imagine we trade bodies with sheep.
We awake one morning with different shaped teeth,
cloven hooves become our hands and feet,
yet we are oblivious, as if we've always been sheep.

Technology changes too with the trade.
Human inventions now look a little strange.
Sheep live with the same untamed desire to innovate.
Adapted for sheepkind, you wouldn't look at hooves the same!

We keep our human brains along with our knowledge.
We eat as normal, go to school, work, college.
Whatever each unique sheep does when leading their own lives,
our human personalities stay embedded in our minds.

With our woven woolly coat,
our ethnicities we keep.
We still have the ability to speak,
drive cars, smoke,
use touchscreens,
look after our pets,
try to peel garlic cloves,
fly planes,
engineer boats,
perform surgery,
write songs, play notes
to create symphonies,
genius music that's therapeutic...
Will we ever live in harmony?

Some sheep might believe in ghosts,
others in aliens, others in both.
Conspiracies always topical,
some truths are undisclosed.
We are creators, teachers, lawyers, scientists,
we search for purpose to exist.

We build bikes, ships, rockets and satellites
in the space race to be the first sheep to capture light.
Is interstellar travel sci-fi or a future possibility?

Politicians still lack the fight to do what's right.
Within the sheep society,
nothing is ever black and white.

Our words, our imaginations,
take us beyond our capabilities.
Searching for answers,
some study Ancient Sheep History.
Others study bacteria in search of cures,
others pull triggers and build nuclear bombs.
We sing New Year songs.

At home, our lambs would chase silhouettes,
if only they spent time outside with their friends...
Instead, they communicate through the internet,
and only play with real toys for seconds.
Naivety beckons
until their eyes are locked to a new screen,
this time it's the TV:
Peppa Pig, Baby Shark and *Shaun the Sheepish Human Being.*

In the Sheep World,
where we work to pay the bills,
where we work to get by,
where we work to put food on the table,
so our lambs' futures are stable,
we push supermarket trolleys around,
hoping for winter to end, so the gas bills go down.
Energy companies raise the price,
wages stay the same, budgets are tight,
we keep the lights off, we struggle to see...

We use candlelight at teatime,
trapped within our wool the smell of burning wax,
we rarely have a shear during winter,
extra-warm blankets coat our backs.

And when we get a chance, we escape the cities.
We drive through the windy lanes, evergreen trees,
quiet streets in the usual Brecon rain,
fleeing to the fields, the fresh air of the countryside,
and as we look out of our windows,
we see human beings, together, on open fields of grass,
surrounded by hedges, some fences, empty roads, parked cars,
happy and relaxed, a part of nature's art.

In one big herd,
free,
with not a worry in the world as we pass...

HOOF TECHNOLOGY 1: HANDY HOOVES

Hoof trainers, hoof high heels,
hoof shoes, hoof boots,
hoof tools,
all fool (hoof) proof,
not all cool though...

Here at Handy Hooves
we have every household tool you'll ever need to use!
Hoof technology integrated into your home living.
We don't want you to work hard,
so we do the hard work for you.
Everything is fitted with bespoke hoofles:
cupboards and drawers, the kettle, the doors.
Place a single hoof in the disc-shaped notch.
There are different sizes to custom-fit you,
suction machines attach to your front two hooves,
to clean the house, called...
'HOOVERS!'
Handy Hooves taps, even Handy Hooves remotes,
and if you can't handle the hooves tools then we'll send a fitter, just for you.
Whatever you need, call 555-44-337 and you'll receive.
Remember:
You're in safe hooves with Handy Hooves

Hoof technology:
new innovative ways for us to live.
Our phones are made a little bigger.

A slick and smooth 360-degree hoofle fitted.
Activate Face ID or hoofprint lock.
Only YOU have access.
Act fast. Low stock.

Discover limitless entertainment
for only £44.99 a month. A real steal!

Or a real piece of junk?

On our cars, our steering wheels fit two circular slots,
no keys to start the engine, just a button to press: start and stop.
All cars automatic – sat-nav, radio, Bluetooth – controlled by
voice.
E-cars will self-drive us to our destination of choice.
No need to concentrate on the road,
artificial intelligence mode, making its own decisions —
statistics show it causes less collisions.

Hoof technology is genius.
Hoof technology is convenient.
Hoof technology is advancing,
creating machines that build skyscrapers,
million-dollar rockets to take the sheep race to Mars,
billions of dollars creating hoof-friendly cars,
hoof watches, hoof computers,
trillions of dollars pumped into new hoof technology!

While millions of sheep around the world are thirsty, hungry.
No access to clean water.
Homeless.
Illegal lamb labour, lambs in need of a saviour,
as the tips of their hooves bleed to meet production needs,
each stitch weaves pain behind the scenes.

A worldwide crisis of sheep in poverty.
A worldwide crisis of sheep inequality.

JOURNAL ENTRY: LONELY

My wool is covering, well, nearly covering my whole face.
I could do with a shave. It's only been three days.
I'm alone in this house. It feels empty.
Knowing I won't see her when I get in from work,
it starts to hurt.
My throat's sore, my legs are heavy,
my forehead is burning up.
My eyes are heavier.
These thoughts are crushing.
When will my mind and body be weightless?

I am alone with my thoughts. I don't feel well.
I know I'm unwell,
I know I need help, I seek help,
but evidently I know it's me who needs to sit here
and figure it out,
how to move on,
how to actually enjoy moments of joy, or just... be,
to take one hoof at a time, just one hoof in front of the next,
one step forward.

I might have pushed my limits too far.
I avoid the drink, I turn to real bars.
The drink makes me feel like somebody else,
the ink makes me —

Feel.

Allows healing.
My cat sits on my lap and licks my wool;
with calming purrs, she looks up at me with love in her eyes —
I am reminded I am not alone.

The chat I had after the gym pops into my mind.
There's something about suffering.
I told the thought-provoked bloke the scenario:
there is beer and there is the gym.
Each are choices to make:
beer with its own path,
the gym with its own path...
If I choose beer then the liquid will release serotonin in my belly,
I most definitely will begin to feel relief and want more.
I most definitely would drink more,
yet the following day I'll suffer.
If I choose the gym,
I will suffer for an hour in physical and mental pain:
physically because my body is working out strenuously,
mentally because my mind is throwing me all sorts of bad thoughts
that distract me.
Yet after the workout is completed,
there is that euphoric feeling...

Seek reward first, then suffer later,
or suffer first and feel the reward after?
The easy or the hard path?
Destructive or constructive?
Long-term pain or short-term pain?
Love myself or hurt myself? Giving in or discipline?
Counterproductive or productive?
Winner or loser?
Weak or strong? Right or wrong?
How do I go on?
I'm writing, but can the page hear me?
Are you listening!

I miss her.

Let me sleep on it.

SHELLY

Shelly is fourteen,
rarely leaves the house to see friends,
rarely sees anybody,
except other sheep on the telly.
Does that count?
She loves the soaps.
Eastenders is her favourite without doubt,
knowing the drama isn't real
is the bubble wrap appeal.
She gets lost in films, a right pretender;
give her a book and she consumes it in days,
sometimes hours,
depending on the genre, of course.
Shelly is just a lover of stories:
love, fantasy, drama, even gory horrors.
Non-fiction is something she avoids,
says it's something about discovering facts that mirror life —
it really makes the wool on the back of her neck stand up.

She hates her parents going to work.
Their commute on the train is unbearable for Shelly.
Sweat trickles from her forehead every morning,
her face turns pale,
heart beats double time.
She chews on her hooves,
pulls out her wool,
until the text comes through.
'I've arrived, enjoy your day sweetheart, try and relax, love you x'

Shelly tries to avoid social media,
thinks its creation has no purpose,
although sometimes the distraction is better than reality.
She watches an influencer called Gabby.

At night, phone in hoof, it becomes a magnet,
a bad habit, scrolling addict,
comparison-damaged.
She only seems to notice
parts on her body
that she hates.
Every change she investigates,
every blemish a flaw,
her mind a menace, she's floored.
Now mirrors make her panicky.
She sleeps twice a day for hours,
every 7pm she showers,
uses soap to wash her face and shampoo for her wool,
by the time she's finished it's time for *Coronation Street,*
with a cup of tea and biscuits as her mum cooks her beige food.

Mondays, however, are the challenge.
The build-up is intense.
Shelly begins to play up,
throwing tantrums, being silly.
Monday is therapy day,
the day unlike the rest.
She is still traumatised from…
well,
I don't want to tell you,
I don't think you'd understand,
or would you?
All the other sheep keep saying
'It's nothing, she needs to just get over it.'
But they don't get it,
never seem to listen…

'She's overreacting. She'll be fine, it's only a sheepish condition.'

THE NEW SHEEK

Welcome, Beautiful Sheep, to the final day in Paris,
for Fabulous Fashion Week!
We have stylists, innovators, artists with a passion for fashion,
and this year's challenge is to define the new 'sheek.'

It's time to bring them out, dressed to impress,
feast your eyes on the unique collection from Dolce & Gabbaa-na.
Fashioned in organic, top-grain Italian,
and designed to be breathable —
a slick approach to gymwear.
Check out those sassy ewes as they strut their stuff.
They look fierce. If looks could pierce your soul!
I always love their synchronised trot, silky swift,
oh, love that, yeah, shake that wool at the end of the stage!
Next, it's the rams, and oh we are fans!
Down the catwalk they smoothly slide, it's as if they're hovering.
They make it look cool, don't they?
I mean, leather gymwear is really reaching,
but don't they make you want to slap it on?
Leatherly!

A lot of applause and awes from that collection!

Up next, it's Ewes Saint Laurent with leopard-skin camo.
Oh, very unoriginal, have we not seen this all before?
Oh, this is a disaster.
The audience don't look impressed, let me tell you.
They look rather disstressed actually,
I mean it is a sight you wish you had *not* seen.

Oh no! A model has had a wobble,
Those hoof high heels. I mean, no wonder! They are enormous!
I'm surprised she can stand let alone attempt a strut.
Oh no, woah, wait! The ewe is down, sheep! The ewe is down!

How embarrassing for her,
Heel snapped by the look of it, awful.
Glad it was only the heel —
and most probably her confidence...
But at least not a broken bone!

Here they are.
I feel sheepish but excited.
They are about to enter the stage.
It is the moment I, and all of you at home, have been waiting for.
Will Baa-berry put a permanent stamp on fashion?
Nobody knows what they're going to come out in,
it's all been so secretive and I'm all for it!
They are about to announce their collection...

Humanistic!
Wow!

The ewes and rams together in force!
Human hair everywhere.
Tassels on boots, pom-pom earrings,
ginger braids at the pits of bomber jackets.
Look at the ewes, they look radiant in those varied colours of
human skin,
Light human-skinned flares go so well with the dark skin beret!
The rams are rocking it,
wearing human nails as chains.
And a little birdie told me
their new skincare range 'Sapien' follows suit,
with their trademark mix of human marrow and sperm.
And I can tell you from experience,
my skin is people-pleasingly soft.
This is revolutionary!
I think this is it!
Humanistic is the new sheek!

THE BARBECUE

Play some tunes at the barbecue,
clap those hooves at the barbecue,
throw some moves at the barbecue,
Barbara's cute at the barbecue.
Ay, Pete, I think I'm gonna make my move.

Sinking beers at the barbecue,
laughter in tears at the barbecue,
the sun is scorching like the barbecue,
got a last-minute fresh trim from Jim,
who let me skip the baa-ber queue.
Finally, I will make my move.

'Pete, come on, we're getting hungry at the barbecue.'
'Food will be two minutes, you can start a queue.'
I get in line next to Barbara, 'Oh, hi, how're you?'
'I'm good, thank you, Bobby, a bit apprehensive about the food.
I'm not a big meat eater and I don't want to be rude.'

'There's no stress, I've been talking to Pete,
he's got veggie sausages to substitute meat.
Although if I were you, I'd give the human a try —
he bought grass-fed, organic breasts, ribs and thigh.
Dip the meat in a little barbecue sauce,
I guarantee your taste buds will be tingling.
Anyway, I've been meaning to catch you,
but I didn't want to intrude as I could see you were mingling...'

'Bobby, I'm sorry, but I'm leaving.
I was trying to be polite,
but I can't stop myself from heaving.
It's not your fault, I... I... don't eat meat for a reason.
I've recently turned vegan,
and seeing the meat cooked has given me a sickening feeling.

The smell of burnt human
is far from appealing.
Tell Pete that I really enjoyed the evening,
but keep this between me and you.
Oh, Bobby, you're so easy to talk to,
such a good friend.
If anybody asks, tell them I forgot
I had something personal to do.
I'll see you in work, have a good weekend.
Enjoy the rest of the barbecue.'

'But, Barbara, you...
I'm sorry I never knew,
I was gonna ask if you...'

JOURNAL ENTRY: THE LOST HUMAN

I feel like the lost human,
I feel like the black human that does not fit in,
judged by the colour of my wool, the shade of my skin.
White sheep say,
'His skin's too dark —
he can't be white.'
Black sheep say,
'He's not black —
his wool's too light.'

How can I fit into a category where I'm accepted?
Different cultures within me are both neglected,
not black enough,
not white enough,
rejected by sheep who call me pale in the winter,
dirty in the summer.

My siblings look different to me,
facial features, colour of wool, colour of skin,
at least I'm not the only one.
I'm fed up with explaining what my heritage is,
as though I *have an obligation* to let them know,
to back up my 'claims' to ethnicity.

I am fed up with feeling judged by black sheep saying I don't belong,
I am fed up with feeling judged by white sheep, who make jokes like,
'Smile, token black sheep, we can't see you in the dark,
black pudding, you can't swim, you've been my nigger from the start.
I'm not racist, just having a laugh.
I mean, surely I can say the word, your kind says it in your raps,
they even named a country 'Niger.' Look, it's on Google Maps.'

HOOKED

Necks bent, stiffened, moulded into a permanent displacement.
Eyes blurry, pupils haunting, eyelids trapped open,
millions of sheep ill, a viral infection.
A pandemic.
Lost.
No connection.
Drool spills from their mouths,
body language talks fragility,
cloven hooves cuddle devices,
the screen, a constant blend of
death,
comedy,
recipes,
gender reveals,
motivation,
gamification,
education,
graduation,
war,
gym,
pranks,
hacks,
bullies,
trolls,
polls,
podcasts,
fake news,
true crime,
ads,
scams,
porn,
opinions,
conspiracies,
weddings,

day-in-the-lifes,
POVs,
unboxings,
travel vlogs,
memes,
DIY,
science,
fashion,
beauty,
tech,
history,
business tips,
self-care,
mental health,
self-improvement,
spirituality,
social experiments,
tutorials,
challenges,
welcome homes,
house tours,
unsolved mysteries,
exploration,
abandoned places,
sports highlights,
cars,
pets,
ASMR,
gaming,
ratings,
reviews,
reactions,
murder.

An addiction.
Sheep are hooked.

LIFTS, GIFTS AND SHIFTS

Sharon runs around,
teeth together, jaw clenched.
I don't mean run as in to keep fit,
no, Sharon is a taxi,
dropping off her lambs for the school run,
out to rugby, football, netball, Brownies,
all sorts of clubs.
Sharon does not stop,
often doing one million and one different things:
getting the lambs up for school,
making tea,
trying to make ends meet
with the little she earns cleaning three times per week,
washing clothes,
while learning accountancy,
working evenings in the local pub.
She barely gets any sleep.

Sharon lifts up her lambs,
gives them the best she possibly can,
pays the rent,
yet has outstanding payments from money lent,
worried there will be none to spend,
but every Christmas, gifts are wrapped in colourful paper,
with pictures on to tell them apart.
Her lambs' faces burst with excitement —
they know their mum's had to work so hard.
Gratitude, hugs,
wrapping their mother in such a tight squeeze
that the lambs' hooves disappear in her coat.
Her son used to think he made her wool curly,
twisting her locks as a lamb.

A super sheep, a super ewe, a single mother,
who uplifts her lambs,
whose gift of love is the greatest gift of all,
and whose resilience shifts away the whispers of other parents
waiting in the car park, outside of the school,
of other sheep who live in the housing association,
who call her names because she keeps herself to herself
and does not associate with anybody else,
all to selflessly protect her lambs,
to not drag them up, but guide them.
Her lambs get the odd comments from teachers,
the postcode watchers,
the assumers,
the jump-to-conclusioners,
but they were brought up to stand up,
to stand out,
to be outstanding.

BAA-BERS SHEAR 1

What can I do for you here, Pete?

Well I need a bit of a shear. How about a high skin-fade?

No worries, coming up. So, how's everything today?

Not bad, not bad, you? Busy?

It's been rammed mate, literally!
Right, this won't take too long,
so, tell me, how's life?
You still working down the road?

Life's a little harder. I wanna quit my job,
but I have a mortgage, I'm a father,
my lambs need a provider...
I don't wanna bore you with the drama.

Noooo, don't be silly, you can tell me anything. I'm your baa-ber.

Well in work, they've not quite been treating me right,
I'm the butt of every joke, they think I'm weak
and they're right.
I've always been intimidated by confrontation.
I don't like to swear or be vulgar in conversation.
I get that other sheep have no filter,
but the filth that baas out of their mouths,
from Phil to Bill to Will to Dyl —
they call it banter.
I'm sick of it, Jim!
To me they're liquorice,
'cause I hate the taste of their words,
I hate the way their racial slurs are cursed.
They're diabolical, a dire species, a new breed, if you ask me.

They say the vilest things when talking about ewes,
all for a laugh, but it's disgusting.

And don't get me started about my shifts,
they're here, there and everywhere, it takes the mick!
Week one, I work seven shifts in a row,
days, nights, weekends with no overtime, what a joke.
Only time in lieu is offered to staff,
but I could do with the extra cash.
My social life has been drained,
no praise in the workplace for what I do.
Week two I only work three days,
but cutting grass all day between graves nearly kills you!

And the weekends there's always unnecessary stress —
poor organisation by my boss, he's not the best.
He brushes off responsibility like dust on a desk,
and that's exactly where he plonks his arse
as he plans what work to give me next.
The latest I've got out of work on a weekend
is nearly two in the morning,
then I had to be back early the next day at half eight to clean,
all day I was yawning.
So, I'm looking for something else that better suits,
something more meaningful with a shorter commute.

Sorry, mate, I've really gone off on one here,
I've just had enough.

No worries at all, my ram!
It's all gravy.
Have a look in the mirror,
I'm all finished with the shear.

JOURNAL ENTRY: BARBELLS, BARS AND BAARS

A decision to be made.
Underneath the barbell is my safe place,
where I can work out all my problems,
where I can lift the sheer weight of the world off my body.
The downward pressure gives me comfort,
I am not broken.
Yet I am starting to be broken down.
I hold the weight,
but I don't know how long I can hold it before I collapse.
I refuse to buckle.
I lower the barbell.
Intrusive thoughts are like dark spells,
rainclouds that never clear,
curses that conjure fear.
When that barbell hits my breast,
I have a choice:
to be crushed,
or to get it off my chest.

I go to the bar when things get hard.
I wish I could just baa it out,
but alcohol fuels me,
it gives me the strength to fight against my mind,
my malevolent intrusive thoughts.
I don't overthink when I overdrink,
it makes me fight
me.
I ended up behind bars before.
I punched a club door,
and broke it.
I know I looked aggressive,
but I was punching the door to hurt my fist,

the pain directed at me.
I ran in front of a taxi.
The dark thoughts were relentless,
as if ten thousand violent screams and shouts,
were all aiming their abuse at me.
I wanted them to be silenced.
The liquid drove me to the middle of the road.
Luckily, I never did too much damage.
I broke the windscreen, smashed my face onto the concrete,
but the next day,
like every next day after too many spirits,
the relief diminished.

After all I have been through,
I come back to you,
poetry,
writing, my therapy,
my escapism,
no,
my reality.
My brain tells my hand,
my hand tells the pen,
my pen tells the page,
and I am free.
Release.

Breathe.

In and out.

I hid it for years in fear other sheep would think I was crazy.
I began writing about my mental health,
about the deep depths of how debilitating each intrusive thought became,
the manipulative persuasiveness was a hook at my mouth,
the bait of compulsion was too hard to resist,
the weight of responsibility it made me feel,
to prevent each intrusive thought from becoming real,
it was mentally paralysing,
mentally traumatising.
I know now that poetry saved my life.
It has been with me from the start,
long before the barbells,
long before the bar —
it is the reason I get out of my bed in the morning.
Now I share my work with the world,
I want them to hear me.
I want to write a book,
something with meaning,
out of the ordinary, intriguing...
After all,
can you silence spoken word, sheep?
Can you silence a lyricist, a wordsmith, a rapper?
Naa,
You, OCD, will never silence these stanzas.
Somebody, please pass me the microphone, drop a beat.
You, Obsessive Compulsive Disorder, will never silence my baars.

SAINTS AND SINNERS

The difference between saints and sinners:

Sheep who are sinners and idolise their desires
to satisfy their wants,
who worship *self* on a shattering shrine,
whose quick-fix pleasures, short-lived,
sacrifice true freedom and peace,
and convince the world to do the same,
think they are saints.

Sheep who are saints,
know they are sinners.

THE FACE OF A FALSE SHEPHERD

A face doesn't need to be coated in paint to be disguised,
it is portrayed in natural ways,
the expressions in the eyes,
the shape of emotion carved as wrinkles
forming uniquely with each squint,
whether it be a hint of joy,
or a blink of concern,
a disguise can break at an uncharacteristic wink.

A sheep can baa the right thing,
portray empathy if a situation calls.
A sheep can be wise,
offer friendly advice,
a warm gentle stroke of the wool of an innocent,
be the role model lambs look up to,
be the sheep other sheep aspire to,
acquire strong relationships,
deep connections,
teach lessons on life to inspire the community.

What if this sheep were a priest,
in a small village,
sworn to celibacy,
sworn to the secrecy of the sins he'd heard?
He is now the Shepherd other sheep follow,
after years and years of service to others,
highly respected because of his morals,
highly regarded as the ram of tomorrow,
as he can solve any problem,
form peace out of quarrels.

Now he's got to the stage
the wrinkles begin to change,
as the act to behave a certain way begins to fade,
an agenda of hostility takes shape,
on the face of a false shepherd,
who takes their aim,
at vulnerable ewes,
ewes who feel disgust, living in shame,
from sins of their past.
He says they're to blame,
'But it's okay to be scared. Life is not a fair game.'
He wipes away tears, sits with them and prays.
'Forgiveness is here, let me show you the way.'
He whispers in their ear, 'Turn around and obey,'
as he pulls down his trousers, leads them astray.
'Do not make a sound until I'm finished, okay?
I promise you'll feel better. Trust me, you're safe.'
Pulls on their wool, they quietly wince in pain,
the wrinkles vanish away,
an evil smile appears, he's captured his prey.
'Now don't go telling the other sheep,
Or your sins will never be washed away.'

THE GRAND CONCERT

Jess: Wow, she really ended with a —

Holly: What!?

Jess: She really ended with a —

Holly: I can't hear you!

Jess: I loved EVERYTHING about that!
Did you see her wool!
She is amazing,
I wish I could get mine done like that!

Holly: What?!

Jess: I said did you see her wool!

Holly: I can't hear you the music's still too loud.
There are too many sheep, it's stressing me out.

Jess: Stay close, grab my wool.

Holly: I need a wee...

Jess: Hurry up, my mum's waiting outside,
plus, we need to talk about what we just witnessed!

...That was quick!

Holly: I didn't go. There was a stupid queue inside,
not worth the wait! It's so busy.

Jess: Quick, this way. My mum said she'd be in reception.
Holly, stay close, don't get lost in the herd like you always do!

Holly: Shush, you.
I'm here, I'm holding on! Just push through.
Oo, shall we buy some merch?
Those t-shirts are crazy!

Jess: No, no, my mum's waiting,
you know it's overpriced here anyway.
Look! There's the door to reception.

Holly: There are so many sheep, it's really stressing me out.
I'm boiling. I am literally like a sponge of sweat.

Jess: Eww, you crazy ewe you.
My first concert and I got to listen to my favourite artist play my favourite song!
Cold! Fire!
I can't wait to tell everybody in school on Monday.

Holly: It's a little cooler here, phew.
Now, where's your mum? Try and find her in this wool madness.

Jess: I have no signal, but she said she'd be in here.
Holly, look at that ram over there.

Holly: Who? Where?

Jess: Over there —
That ram with the massive backpack on,
He looks so...

...

Headteacher: Jess and Holly were not just pupils at this school,
they were kind, caring and loved dearly by their friends.
This school will eternally miss their laughter,
their bubbly personalities, and their drive to succeed,
letting nothing step in their way.

It has been revealed that this violent act of terrorism was by a
young ram, part of a radicalised group,
but we want to make clear that this school will not tolerate
Islamophobia.
We want sheep to pull together during this awful tragedy.
We can not let this divide us or break us.
We are stronger if we support each other as one herd.
If you, or if any sheep you know,
need any help to get through this,
then please talk to your teachers
and we can support you.
We will be holding a memorial for Jess and Holly on Friday
here at the school.
Whoever wants to attend, please do.

HYPOCRITE

Sheep gather round,
signs held between clenched hooves,
protestors baa and baa the same old tune:
'We want them out, so why let them in!'
On the news, the nation is listening.

It's raining heavily,
cold droplets soak wool.
No sheep shiver,
no sheep shake the water off their backs
that begins to weigh them down.
Blood is boiled.
The atmosphere is heated —
you can taste the tension.

But first...
it's time for a break
after rallying for two hours.

The smell of the Indian takeaway opposite. Irresistible.

A homely feeling, as the warm spices slip down the throat.

Some sheep are burning,
sweat soaks their wool.
Panic.
Desperate to get home,
rejected, caught in the Greek fires.
They are screaming, aggravated, aggressive, stressed.
Some get arrested.
No public transport, no planes.
They have these entitled looks on their faces,
yet try to play innocent.
'We just want to go home and be safe.
Show us you care, show us mercy, show us an escape.
Let us back in.
Get us out of here,
please,
we are scared.
I am scared for my lamb's life.
Are you listening?
Have you no sheepanity?
Please help us escape.
But we are British.
Listen to me!'

HYSTERIA

Sheep misheard
Sheep, mis herd

Why are you taking away our voices?
Why won't you hear our baas?
Why are you eliminating our choices?
Why do you judge us by our class?
Why do you make it hard for us to protest?
Why do you put us all in the same category?
Why do you threaten arrest?
Why do you refuse to listen to our stories?
Why do you not see the signs?
Why do you take no notice?
Do you not want the sheep to rise?

As your wage increases and the living wage freezes,
your focus, purely capital,
is mass sheep control.
We need a leader we can console in,
not some sheep who plays with our lives,
who spreads fear, far and wide,
the parasite of diseases:
Hysteria.

The symptom that eases pleasure
from your egotistical minds,
implying to sheepkind 'You need us,'
but after the herd see through your lies,
we realise, we are already blessed without your sneezes.

Why do you think you understand
when you're oversaturated with greed?
Why are your wants a definitive demand
when you've overlooked our needs?
Why do you impede impactful plans?
You can't keep up with our working-class speed.

Why do your promises always disintegrate?
What does power never want to be challenged?
Why do you hesitate?
Innovate.
Create a land where ordinary sheep are free, are heard,
the ones who know what it's like to suffer and work.

Why are you not listening to all the baars
of the artists who advocate for change?
Why is creativity not a lead member of your staff?
Imagination is invaluable, is that why you see it as strange?

We are drained from being misheard,
and misrepresented.

We are drained from being mis herd.
Will you ever represent us?

Your plan to make us fight amongst ourselves:
a demented incentive.

STRINGS

Pulling strings,
controlling things that shape society.
Puppetting the sheeplic
are puppeteer politicians,
who continue to pull the wool over our eyes,
as we have little choice in government decisions,
misguided, mis herd, as we are forced to follow in a flocky mess,
knowing that we never really get to decide.
With power, division will always exist,
because segregation is the only way they know how to make everything fit.
Separation will always come before equality –
equality's a myth,
as greed overrides everything.
Are we too sheepish to stand up to the ancient way in which our
society lives?

Freedom of speech — is it an impossible feat?
Every word has a consequence.
To speak out against the injustice of the world in peaceful protests,
has a consequence.
Brutal arrests,
forced by police.
Who are they working for? Are they keeping the peace?

True freedom of travel, to be nomads,
has been ripped from our instinctive hearts,
every sheep territory controlled,
refugees terrified by terror,
refused entry to safer lands,
borders locked, borders blocked, borders open to certain flock,
but the Lion keeps his eye on this flock by night.
Welcomes them in, to display empathy –
yet is prepared to send them away indefinitely,
if a single hoof steps out of line.

GABBY

Gabby takes thousands of snaps a day
documenting the perfect parts of her lifestyle.
She prides herself on being a 'real ewe.'
Her 200,534 followers consist of young lambs,
mainly ewes under the age of 16.
Gabby is 28. She dropped out of university.
Her job?
An influencer,
taking her further than her Geography degree,
promoting products she doesn't use,
oblivious to the potential harm they cause,
the chemicals that react with the skin.
They give the script, she plays along.
Now the money's coming in.
She doesn't really understand what they do, how they work,
the payment and sponsorship all seems worth it –
no wonder she quit her degree.
What a privilege, what an opportunity
to work with an up-and-coming skincare company.
The ultimate boost to her profile!

She spends all her time online,
or in the mirror,
ever since somebody commented,
'Ewwwwe, you are so pasty pale,
disgusting to look at,'
even though her followers
jumped to her defence,
called out the hate,
reassured Gabby that she is beautiful,
the comment stuck out like a sore cloven hoof.

Now she wakes at 5am every morning,
ensuring her image is pristine, her daily routine.

Her goal?
To make every post go viral,
show young lambs how to be a 'real ewe.'

BODY FAST

Wait, wait, wait, wait, wait!
Stop scrolling!
If you want to know the secret recipe to burning stubborn fat,
all you need to do is watch this 60-second video.

I've been testing out training programs
combined with evidence-based nutrition,
and the exact sleep pattern you need,
to lose body fat, **FAST!**
Welcome to **BODY FAST**
where we help sheep like you,
get the body you deserve!
But you must act now.
We are giving the first 100 sheep who sign up,
NOT 20%,
NOT 30%,
NOT EVEN 50%,
but a STAGGERING
90% OFF
our 5-week program.

We guarantee you will lose body fat, fast,
without having to intermittent fast,
without having to skip breakfast,
without having to give up fast food!

The formula is just a click away,
want to know more?
Sign up today
and live a body fat-free life.
So, fasten your seatbelts,
You're about to go on a ride that I know will change your life!
BODY FAST will decrease your appetite,
no need to have a bite.

Call that **BODY FAST** food.
Better mood!
More energy,
less mass,
forget lethargy.
You will be able to go about life
leaner,
fitter,
faster.
There is no better-tested formula.
Forget the fat past,
subscribe today and get the body you deserve at lightning speed,
with little effort.
This is
BODY FAST.

JOURNAL ENTRY: INFINITE VERSIONS

There are literally infinite variations of me,
of this sheep —
the way I look, act, sound, in this exact moment.
Or at least that's what science says.

The multiverse:
multiple realties,
multiple versions of me,
infinite decisions,
infinite choices,
forming infinite actions,
leading to infinite, individual chain reactions,
equalling the future, equalling who we are
and who we have chosen to be,
formed,
even by the minute, atom-sized, almost involuntary decisions,
such as, whether to get out of bed or not —
No, that's too vague…
I don't know,
you know, the autopilot things we do like going to the toilet —
bad example.
But let me continue through this journaling time-continuum.

I mean literally every single thing we do, forms a sequence,
a pattern,
which determines our future,
which has consequences.
Our choices create sequences
and every choice has a consequence,
meaning, there is the same sheep (being me),
out there in the multiverse,
writing this exact journal.

But they might end it differently,
causing a new sequence.
Maybe there are also clones of me in other universes?
Infinite versions of me,
infinite clones of me.
Maybe I'm a human being in another universe?
That would be rather mad.

Scientists have already cloned the first human being.
If they clone something biological,
that must mean they can clone sheep as well?
It all baffles me, this stuff,
but I love it.
I love opening the cranium
and allowing imagination
to roam freely and lead me somewhere unexpected,
like here,
a stream of infinite consciousness,
jotted down in infinite journals,
with infinite possibilities and infinite consequences,
that coincidentally lead back to me.

They even named the human clone.
They called her Dolly.

BARISTA

Bobby: Here you go, an americano with oat milk.

Barbara: Goat milk? Oh no, I can't drink goat milk.

Bobby: No I said oat, oaaaaat milk. Haha.

Barbara: Ohhhh, sorry, I completely misheard you.
I panicked for a second then! What did you get?

Bobby: An americano, black. Trying to reduce my calories.

Barbara: Why? You look in good shape to me!

Bobby: Oh, don't flatter me!
Anyway, how are you since the barbecue?

Barbara: Oh, I'm fine.
Sorry about that, I just cannot do the meat thing.

Bobby: No, no, don't apologise it's cool, I get it. Every sheep has
their 'sheep thing' you know, our preferences tailored to us.

Barbara: Oh, I love that.
But just for your reference, it goes deeper than just food.
When I was in uni, me and the girls would go out to this bar called Rude.
It was quirky, had crazy music and stayed open from 5pm until
12pm the following afternoon.
We would go there for dinner and stay there and drink.

Anyway, this one time there was a group of rams
who would not take the hint.
They kept swarming us, making jokes, getting too close,
could not accept defeat.
All night they did this on repeat.

It got really late.
They were drooling like they wanted something to eat.
They made us feel super uncomfortable —
they looked at us like we were slabs of meat.

That image is imprinted on my mind,
along with animal rights,
climate change, after that I went vegan.
I guess it was a sign.

Bobby: Oh my days. That is shocking.
Some rams just do not understand when to move on —
they build their own coffin.
I want you to know that I'm not like any of those rams.
I hope you know not all rams are bad, and although I must admit,
I was over the moon when you agreed to meet,
I do find you attractive, but I want to get to know you, what's underneath.
I know you don't have much time today, but it's been nice just to chat and have a coffee.

Barbara: Oh, Bobby, you're making me blush, you are very sweet.
How about next time the drinks are on me?...

Bobby: Yes, why not! How about next week?

Barbara: See you then!

(Barbara leaves. Bobby runs up to the barista, whispers.)

Bobby: Could you put some goat milk in my coffee, please?

SHEEPANE

Humans crammed in dens,
next to hens.
The small ones eaten by foxes in the night,
the weak ones taken by Hand, Foot and Mouth, lost the fight.
Mass-bred, mass-fed.
Corn to make them plump.
Pumped with medicines, preservatives, bodies dumped
on the back of the gigantic tractor trailer,
the noise is unbearable as they crush each other,
biting the air for oxygen, survival of the strongest,
the ones with the longest limbs, the ones that are slim,
the sponges, who absorb everything, often suffocate,
but if any are part of a family, special treatment awaits.

They are guided together in a separate truck,
to the slaughterhouse.
What?
You forgot?
Sheep are sheepane, you know,
allowing humans to let all the water out.

Tears burst from the father human's eyes
as he watches his young son,
daughter, and mother of his children, being dragged by the neck.
Screams pierce ear drums,
shock and reality sweep them off their feet.
He chases after, blood leaks from his ear —
it's half torn off.
His naked body covered in bruises, and what looks like mud.
His tears bathe him, as they blend into the rain.
A dark night for a night of pain.

Two sheep chase after the human with dogs.
The human bursts through the slaughterhouse doors,
buckling his knee.
He crawls towards his beloved family.
They reach for him, cry for him,
but are locked in iron chains.
The dogs catch up and bark loudly in his face.
They do not bite.

The first sheep enters with a smug look on his face,
'I know you want to see your family,
so, we will let you,
now watch.'

The sheep orders the slaughter —
a larger sheep with spades as hooves, a muscular physique,
and a beer belly,
walks in with an axe.
'Which one first?' he calls.
'The little ones, son then daughter.
Leave the mother last.'
The human man, now on all fours, cries out loud,
as the taste of iron enters his mouth.

THE FARM

The farm is where all the sheep flock to when in need,
when sheep bleed, have a virus, a disease,
the farm is open —
come and see.

Cara waits, nibbling her hoof,
with her one good tooth,
her eyes shadowed by a frown,
a single tear trickles down,
lands on her patches of knotted wool,
lonely, empty, full of the if, the what if, the wait.

Another 2 hours of pain,
she was ensured that she has the **best** treatment *available* —
the **best** treatment *unavailable*, too costly,
yet it would save Cara from suffering.

Each sheep unsure of the way of the system,
money makes the world go around, currency has tricked them.
Healthcare, a hierarchy of medication:

> Barely alive.
> Fairly alive.
> Probably survive.
> Cure?
> No regulations.

It's the cure everybody is chasing,
Or is it the cure somebody is erasing?
On a farm, factories make foods with preservatives
that have shown links to cancer cells;
the same farm, using the same factories,
provides the treatment for metastasis.

Diseases, illnesses, sheep addicted to additives,
sedatives, sheep asleep, dead, yet they live.
Natural land, herbs as medicine are laughed at,
crazy if you think a plant could fight back.
Medicines only relevant on prescription,
each with a similar-looking description.

'Our remedies are energy destroyers.
They need to stay on medicines for life, for our employers.
Keep the sheep barely alive. They need to know us,
so they can grow us — our company will blow up.
We are not a farm at all. We don't even like the sheeplic.
We like the smell of cash.
We invite sheepkind to keep eating junk and keep getting ill.
We will manufacture your new life, with a pill.'

Cara waits eagerly as The Farm drama takes place —
sheep queuing up, patients impatiently chase
a medication to help them feel less insane,
waiting for the Big Farmer to take their pain away.

JOURNAL ENTRY: SUPERPOWERS

If I could choose my own superpowers,
I would shoot amazing webs,
climb walls,
do crazy-cool flips,
my strength, spectacular —
I would catch moving vehicles.
My sense would tingle and time would dwindle,
as I react quicker than the speed of sound.
I'd disguise myself as a nerd,
dress smart, plain shirts,
taking pictures for the local paper,
I would be no paper chaser,
but a masked hero, chasing villains,
catching them in my web,
throwing away the venom,
the vultures, the goblins of my city,
Cardiff,
where artists paint murals on city corners of heroes,
where I target injustice with my web shooters,
jumping with euphoria from building to building,
and when the *Avengers* visit me,
I will not hesitate to help save this planet from all of its
destruction,
I will shake the hand of Ironram and say,
'Yes,
I will join you on this mission,
this mission to save the city,
the World, the Universe.

I am not just your friendly neighbourhood hero,
oh no,
I am Spider-Ram.'

HOOF TECHNOLOGY 2: TOOLS

In the olden,
the golden,
the stoic,
the heroic days,
tools were made to last.
If you needed a spade to dig up your lawn,
it would be made from the strongest metal,
welded so well, that snapping the hoofle was never an aggravation.
A washing machine could hit twenty years and still be spinning.
A well-oiled machine on four wheels
would still get you from A to B,
even if it reached its predicted lifespan.
Tools were tougher,
machines built to be robust.

They just don't make them how they used to.

New hoof technology has a short expiration.
Hoofles of spades crack and snap,
washing machine parts break and collapse,
car parts – cheap, never intact –
as MOTs fail,
cars break down,
their parts useless,
even though they were used less.
How is this a thing?

It makes no sense.

We live in the age of advanced hoof technology,
yet the majority made is poor quality.
Or if you want top of the range,
then you really have to pay for it,
aim high.

But that's the issue,
the problem,
it's the smooth back and forth smug rub of the cloven hooves,
'Card, cash or bank transfer?'
The more that's made, the more the companies sell,
the more they sell, the larger the profit,
more money.

They need things to break,
they need consumers,
to constantly consume.
They craft hoof tools
with just enough strength,
so they last just enough time
for the counting sheep to justify buying another.
If not,
they have a tool hierarchy:
the more money you pay,
the better in shape your tool will stay.

The world is currently screaming about climate change,
how wasteful we are as a sheep society,
yet governments allow poor products to be made
to boost our sheep economy.

If we all supported each other and money did not divide,
hoof tools would be made to last.

They have created the lightbulb that will never go out,
but refuse to release it...

I wonder why that is.

BAA-BERS SHEAR 2

Alright, Jim, you got time for a quick trim?
Or should I say, quick shear?

Come on in, Pete!
The seat's free. Give me a minute to sweep up the wool.

...

So, what can I do for you?

Just short back and sides please, Jimmy.

No worries. So, how's things?

Not bad, Jim, not bad. You?

Alright thanks, Pete, my ram, alright.

You been affected by this cost-of-living joke?

I have mate, but haven't we all?
I wanted to put the prices up,
but how will I get the sheep through the doors?
I'll lose my customers, Pete.
I will just have to put up with being a little less well off, you know.

Oh, Jim, put your prices up, will you,
we all need to look after ourselves in this mess,
the disgusting mess the Wolves have put us in —
and the Sheep Dogs pretend to address.
You know what, the last 10 years or so it's been going downhill,
quicker than a wheel of cheese.

Yes, the country is looking a bit blue.
The Wolves with their misguided stories,
the Sheep Dogs with their tails between their legs.
Not a backbone in sight,
but the thing is sheep fall the propaganda
the media spams on every screen.
Take a look at this clip. They're glorifying their roles.
Go on, have a proper gander.

Sheep unfortunately, in this day and age, are gullible.
They follow like a flock of humans.
First it was this Brexit crap,
then that sheep, what's his name, quit,
coward.
They've been caught with offshore accounts,
and have the cheek to tell us to pay tax.
COVID… let's not talk about that.
Parties at Number 10,
taking the mick out of the whole nation,
while we were mourning.
Joke.
Then the ram whose Mrs is minted,
yet loves a cheeky tax dodge, comes in,
and this ram thinks he understands the working class.
My ar…

Ask yourself this, Pete,
who are they benefitting, and why?
Because it's not the working class.

I know.
The cost of living's nearly killed us, Jimmy!
Food's flown up, everything's flown up.
We are walking on two hooves here,
trying to balance our lives.
BP oil, did you hear, made 7 billion last year?
Gas prices are about to explode.

We must look at it like this though, Pete:
at least we have a home to go to,
a roof over our heads.
There are those out there now
who are in survival mode,
wishing they were here.
We need to appreciate what we have.

Frankly this next election I really am stuck on who to vote for,
I trust none of them.
The far left, the far right, it's all a mess.
You know what I say, Jimmy?

Go on...

I say a bird has to have a left wing and a right wing to fly.
Balance is what we need, my ram, balance.
I agree with bits on that side and bits on the other.
Maybe we need to find the middle ground.

On that note, turn to your side,
Have a look in the landscape mirror.
Short back and sides.

Legend.
Here you go, Jimmy, have an extra quid.
Take care, see you soon my ram!

FORMAL RAP BATTLE:
THE WOLVES VS THE SHEEP DOGS

THE WOLVES

Just in case you forget, we are the Wolves.
We can secretly eat the sheep, just leave you with the wool.
You talk about showing our true colours, don't judge us,
we just love to watch all the poor sheep suffer,
while we sit and sip away on a hot, sweet cuppa,
in front of the fire, baaing out loud,
we are mean sheep suckers,
rowdy and proud.

What?
We don't have the *energy* to pay for the gas hike —
electricity, specifically, we get for half price.
Install our log burners — all the trees, we'd burn them all.
Stop blaming us for these luxuries you can't afford.
Get up off your lazy hooves,
buy some tidy shoes,
get out there on the road.
There are loads of jobs, but the sheeplic moan.
So, we don't care about their bones,
we don't care about their meat.
One day they'll cry wolf,
panic amongst the streets.
They'll need order, so us Wolves will begin to preach:
we have your best interest at heart,
but we don't want to hear a peep.
We're not soft like you Sheep Dogs.
We are prepared to teach
a very harsh lesson to the noncompliant sheep.
We'll arrest if they protest.

Send immigrants back to sea.
They want to fight global warming, but lack the tenacity,
lack the guts, the nuts and the lung capacity
to perform an impactful speech —
dirty scum need fags to breathe.
Get these sheep freaks some handcuffs please.
Why don't they understand?
This all about power —
the money and the land is not theirs, it is ours.
But you silly Sheep Dogs keep putting things in their heads.
If that's how you want to play it, we will eat you too —
you'll wind up dead.
And we will use your wool to pull over the sheeplic's eyes.
We may be sheep too, but we are Wolves in disguise.

THE SHEEP DOGS

We work around the clock, we never sleep, never stop.
Tick tock, on Big Ben's time, we're on TikTok, follow and watch.
We tackle the big jobs, 24/7 lead our flock.
We are for the Sheep, we adore the sheep. Woof woof!
We are the Sheep Dogs.

Let's talk about the cost of living,
a toxic prison,
forget your fancy boots on your cloven hooves,
we wanna know the truth, whose socks you filling?
We got sheep, naked, barely living,
afraid to put on the heating,
a choice between warmth and eating,
their woolly coats are not enough to keep them from freezing!
While your offshore accounts avoid tax, you are cheating,
but somehow get away with it. This is unfair treatment.
You see it's not about the golden money tokens,
it's about the ones in your arms you were holding.
So, this Christmas let us make a wish,
that all sheep have enough warmth and food to live.
We are for the many, you are for the few,
you don't know what it's like
to not have enough money to support your ewe,
or your ram, or even your little lambs.
The working class work off their arse
and you don't give a damn,
when at the end of the week,
their pay barely covers the fees,
the rent and council tax,
forget gas, just pay the electricity.
We are in a city who elected you.
It was a mistake because all you do is electrocute.
Who is the Lion, please?
I mean, the next Lion, please?

All the Wolves keep on resigning,
you leave us in jeopardy.
Pathetic an enemy.
I don't have the *energy*
to explain what that's meant to mean.
But ever since you've been in power,
this place is on its back,
four legs kicking in the air while you sing and drink, kickback.
You're like a song with no melody,
narcissists need therapy,
if we had telepathy, we'd give you all the penalties,
that you'd mentally serve, for all your crimes.
Why is climate change barely on your mind?
Do you want us to die?
The sheep race on its way to extinction,
you don't flutter an eye,
lid on the jar of the jam,
you're sour, that's part of the plan.
You won't let the sheep protest
(but neither will we),
instead you arrest a disruptive ewe and ram.
The sheeplic are closing in on you,
exposing the truth,
holding you accountable,
but I told them to prepare for an attack.
Beware, watch your back.

We spot a wolf, dressed in sheep's clothing.

TURN A BLIND EYE

Turn a blind eye
You have no prerogative.

Turn a blind eye
The lambs were wearing clothes quite provocative.

Turn a blind eye
Yes, there were many rapes.

Turn a blind eye
But you're being Islamophobic in this case.

Turn a blind eye
Everything is sexualised.

Turn a blind eye
None of this is contextualised.

Turn a blind eye
We now know it's quite prevalent in the media.

Turn a blind eye
How you try to cause hysteria.

Turn a blind eye
No, in fact, you are wrong.

Turn a blind eye
Nobody knew it was going on.

Turn a blind eye
The Director General was oblivious.

Turn a blind eye
Well... those emails are quite insidious.

Turn a blind eye
High profile lifestyle is quite stressful.

Turn a blind eye
It was entertainers, news reporters, presenters in general.

Turn a blind eye
Why are you pressing me?

Turn a blind eye
They will destroy my career, in the press, you see.

...

Turn a blind eye
Yes. there were cover-ups.

Turn a blind eye
Yes, many lambs, yes, that runner, up.

Turn a blind eye
I know, I'm sorry, it was disgusting.

Turn a blind eye
Images and videos among the corruption.

Turn a blind eye
You don't know the half of it.
It's rife, kept in the dark. If lit,
the system will collapse.

The victims have no chance.

TREASURE ISLAND

Now my lovely lambs, when we get to Treasure Island,
I need you all to be on your best behaviour.
Are you all excited to go on this adventure!

                                                    Yes, sir!

When the boat pulls in, you will be allocated an adult,
either an ewe or a ram,
if you're lucky you might get the Prince!
You must go with them to find the treasure,
you must do exactly what they ask,
you don't want to miss out, do you?

                                                    No, sir!

If you find the treasure on this adventure,
you will be invited to something very special,
The White Party!
Now, has everybody got their bags of toys they are taking with
them?

                                          Three bags full, sir!

NEWS REPORT: 'LAMB SHANKED'

It happened on a well-known London street
in the early hours this morning.
CCTV shows a young ram, intoxicated,
walking towards the taxi ranks,
a gang of three followed him,
one holding a machete.
What happens next
is one of the most vicious attacks in knife crime history,
the solo young ram was ambushed,
pushed with force in the back, to the floor,
and stabbed repeatedly for an entire minute,
with a total of 95 stab wounds to the flesh.

The following footage contains distressing images.
The gang initially target the young ram's legs,
then begin random violent slashes with the blade
as the three young rams who formed the gang shared the weapon.

The young ram was left to die, alone,
until an early morning jogger stumbled upon a pool of blood and
flesh.

The attack was brutal and calculated.
The police are now talking with witnesses
who heard an argument the solo ram had,
with the gang of three,
in the smoking area of the nightclub THRILLER
just minutes before the attack,
where the young ram, only 18 years old, was seen,
protecting his friend from his future assailants.

The gang have all been arrested and are in custody,
set to go straight to court.
This is not the first of these brutal attacks.
Knife crime has been on the rise in the UK.
Statistics show the sheeplic are becoming desensitised to violence.

Later we will be talking to the Minister for Crime and Policing
to ask again,
what is the government doing to prevent knife crime?

I'm Anita Victor.
Back to you in the studio.

JOURNAL ENTRY: WALES VS ENGLAND

Atmosphere
Goosebumps
Butterflies
Teary eyes
Fireworks
Anthems
Passion
Dragons
Energy
Lightning
Flames
Fierce
Power
Strength
No fear
Stoic
Entertaining
Igniting
Game face
Game on
Kick off!

The Welsh against the English in the Principality Stadium,
where heroes are born
in a war that turns rams to legends.

What a game it was!
The fly half's kicking was on top-notch form,
slotting penalties, making conversions, kicking for touch,
The golden hoof of Wales.
The destructive force of the forwards
battling every scrum, every ruck,

tackles, injuries, hand-offs.
They left their blood, sweat and wool on that pitch.
And the backs, well they broke their backs on that field,
between the powerhouse centres and the sidestepping wingers,
it is beyond me,
it absolutely baffles me,
how these rams move so swiftly and quickly
on two legs,
with the ball cradled in their front two hooves,
wild.
They almost looked like they were Humans!
The balance of them, well,
there was no balance from me
or anybody else in the stands as fans,
at least from what I could see.
Everybody else was getting legless or were already there!
I was sitting next to some English sheep, they love the banter,
started calling us the typical Welsh,
the human being-bangers,
I shouted back, we bang 'em you eat 'em!
They laughed it off.
You see unlike in other sports,
opposition fans,
seem to get along in rugby,
even though we support different sides,
we are united by the game.
There was hardly a peep from them after,
holding their heads in shame,
a sea of sheep in red engulfing the spots of sheep in white with
dragon flames,
we were victorious in the battle,
we won this war,
the derby,
what an atmosphere.
The roof was closed!

JOURNAL ENTRY: THE GRAND CANYON

Wow, either this was an extremely big explosion or a huge meteor.
Either way the shock waves
must have set ripples through the fabric of gravity,
across the entire Earth, 'cause this is a mighty hole.

The Grand Canyon.

It was probably caused naturally, actually.
Our catastrophe of a comic bus guide
possibly told us that at some point,
on the excruciating three-hour journey to get here.
I don't for the life of me remember what that ram was on about,
I switched off in the end,
just wanted a peaceful ride and to see the scenes,
me and my mates ended up making jokes out of him!
He was awful
trying to crack jokes when we were at the Hoover Dam,
'The Hoover Dam was created by sheep
whose hooves sucked the life out of the job'
Awful...
No excuse.
Poor execution.

With all that said, it was still such a cool experience
being at both spots.
It was totally crazy driving up towards Arizona.
The desert was snowing!
Blew my mind!
Oh no, I feel myself picking up some American lingo,
I've only been here three days
with not long to go until we all catch our flight back home,
which sucks.

Anyway, The Grand Canyon was massive for me,
a gigantic tick off the bucket list.
I got one of my friends to record me performing
a part of this poem I'd started,
part of a larger project I'm still figuring out.

The Grand Canyon,
although intimidatingly high when looking down —
the Hoover Dam freaked me right out in comparison,
as we walked along the thick concrete wall
which came up to our chests,
the only thing that stood between us
and imminent death.

We heard the news this morning,
about Russia invading Ukraine,
it feels impossible,
it feels surreal,
it makes me ask myself what would I do in that situation?
How would I protect those I love and hold close?
I feel so sorry for the innocent sheep of Ukraine.
Their homes now a war zone,
buildings blown up,
sheep literally dying and I'm here on a Stag Do
getting boozy in Las Vegas.
Insane.

Last night we were woken by an alarm.
It sounded like an air raid.
An ewe with no emotion in her voice
told us to remain calm and stay in our rooms.
Two rams got in an argument down the other end of the strip.

It got bad, one of them was shot.

AUCTION

Now then, this item is from the 16th century.
Sheep used it to straighten their wool.
Instructions:
Place two heated iron plates parallel
then firmly squish the wool together,
gently move your arms away from the body.

We will start the bid at £20,
anybody for £20?
Do I see a buyer, £20?

Baa Baa Baa

You, sir, there we have you.
£25 anybody?
Unique item this,
come on, come on,
this is not Bargain Hunt,
I thought this was a prestigious auction!

Online bidder for £30?
Lovely,
and 5
40
And 5
50
And 5
60
70
80
90
100
Noooo, are you sure?
No more online bids?

We have it. £100 in the room,
I am going, once,
I am going twice,
and done.
Sold to you, sir, in the front row.

Next up, we have a collector's item,
iron chains, branded by the company
Mutton Metal.
Early 19th century, this.
Not sure what these particular chains were used for,
but in good nick nonetheless.
We have neck chains and hoof chains.
Can I start the bid at £900?
Straight at the back,
£950
online now £1000
middle row £1100
and £1500,
and £2000
and 3000
4000 shouts the ewe at the back,
and 5
and 55
and 6
7
8
£10000 shouts the ram in the leather jacket!

Is that it?
Anymore for anymore?
I am going to make the sale.
Last chance
and...
it's all yours, sir,
neck and hoof chains from the 19th century!

The ram in the leather jacket takes his chains and leaves,
on to the next auction,
a private invite-only auction.

He pulls up outside an old run-down pawn shop,
as he enters, he puts his pistol into a bag.
He is guided downstairs by two beautiful ewes.
The place lights up, alcohol flowing, cocaine, a mist in the air.
A smiley, charismatic chap jumps onto the stage.

Welcome, my very special guests.
Today's auction will not disappoint
we promise to satisfy your needs.

Let us bring out the line-up.
We have young lambs,
not yet tried and tested, fresh,
for a solid price,
remember they are reusable so treat them well.

Baa baa baa

Cough up your price.
They are cute, they are pretty.
Shall we begin?

BUYER

lamb, you are mine,
please, there is no need to be afraid,
just close your eyes,
there is nowhere to run away,
take my hoof, stay inside,
touch my thighs,
unbuckle my belt,
lay on the bed, don't you call for help,
that's it, silence, the sound of obedience,
after this you will please my friend,
but remember you are my favourite,
behave until the end,
and I will make sure you get fed,
make me money, stay in my bed,
you are mine.

LITTLE LAMB

Mary had a little lamb,
her fleece as white as snow,
born far too early,
not enough time to grow,
placed in an incubator,
sent straight to ITU.
Mary sick with infection,
her body battered and bruised.

She feared for her lamb,
worried a bond would not form,
she never knew the dad,
which seemed out of the norm,
said she was a virgin,
her parents upset, concerned,
the Doctor called them in to talk,
'Be prepared for what I've learned,
For I am sure it will come as a shock,
The DNA of the lamb has been tested.'
'Please, doctor, what is it?'
'Here are the results...
Incest is suggested.'
The parents could not speak,
looked each other in the eyes,
a sudden realisation,
a shiver up the spine,
as they turned to the window,
muttered, 'It cannot be.'
Staring at Mary's brother,
who was waiting patiently.

Mary soon recovered,
but was in complete distress,
as her parents had signed papers,
to take care of all the mess.

Social workers took her little lamb,
for a fostered family to raise.
You see, Mary was a little lamb,
only twelve years of age.

BAA-BERS SHEAR 3

Back again?

Aye, back again.

How you been?

Stressed as usual, you know how it is,
no rest for the working class!

What we avin'? Same as usual?

No, I tell you what, just shave it all off!

You sure?

Shave it all off.

You are joking?

No, number 1 please, all off. Like the old days.
No more calling me shaggy...

Who's calling you shaggy?

Those melons in work, Jim.
I turn a blind eye, I can have a bit of banter,
but they go on and on.
I don't want to get involved,
but this is the exact reason why they see me as a target.
Too passive, too weak.
Or at least that's what they think.
Then I bite,
and they don't like it when I bite.

What did you do?

Nothing but spoke my mind. They give it but can't take it, end of.

Taking the mick, I can't deal with stupid lazy rams
who have nothing better to do than moan.
I was born with no middle ground —
middle lamb syndrome. And a sin it is, I tell you.
I am either passive,
where they walk their dirty four little legs all over me,
or I bite.
As I said, this time, I bit.

I have enough going on, worrying about Shelly,
trying to figure out what's going on with her mental health,
while keeping her mother calm,
I'm not even with the ewe anymore! But I do care for her.
I lost it when they had the cheek to say
I need to keep better control of my Diabetes.
They don't have a clue.
They don't know the difference
between Type 1 and Type 2, for a start.
The cheek, I was fuming!
I try and treat myself quickly when I go low.
I don't even wait the full twenty minutes to get back to work —
sometimes I know I'm having a hypo,
yet I keep on grafting away in desperate need of glucose.
I feel like I'm in survival mode,
Those fools think I'm slacking,
no matter how many times I try to educate them.

I lost it.
I quit my job.
Just shave it all off,
I won't be able to afford the next shear.

Sorry, mate, they sound like right idiots.

SHELL

Over time the sharp, jagged edges of rocks, change.
They become smooth, shaped in no pattern but their own.
Small, large, heavy, light, pretty, dull,
pebbles at the seaside.

Shelly picks up a small grey pebble, reaches up towards the sky,   *inhales*
then throws it into the sea, as far as her strength allows,   *exhales.*

I love searching for creatures on the beach.
Under rocks, I often find crabs,
usually hiding out in their own little rock pools,
their own escape,
their own getaway from the sea, and the other creatures.

It's hard running on the pebbly beach on two hooves.
I often crawl.
My wool weighs me down when I get wet from the rain
and the splashes from the rock pools.

This is how I discovered the real meaning of my name.
Neither Mum nor Dad get it,
but I know I was named for a reason.
Every name has a meaning, right?

When I crawl, I can see up close tiny patterns on miniature shells,
each pattern,
just like the pebbles,
are unique.
Some pebbles have fossils,
some have shells that are alive and kicking,
minding their own business,
away from the rest,
just like the crabs,
yet protected by their shell.

That is why my name is Shelly.
I was meant to discover this,
and the seaside,
my place of rest,
my escape from the noise,
the pressure,
alone,
safe,
quiet.
My place to understand my strengths.
My place to learn that I have an invisible shell protecting me.

Every moment like this,
I conquer —
the jagged edges I have,
over time I will smooth them out,
I will come out of my shell,
but for now,
I am learning how to do that.

UPSET

The olden ways were much less complicated.
I miss the days of getting into bed,
staring at the ceiling,
being at one with my imagination.
When I was a lamb I used to dream about what the future held.
I was excited about my next day at school,
I would use my mind, my vision,
to picture how things would go.
It felt like a superpower,
then I would dream.

Nowadays,
lambs go to bed with their tablets,
their phones,
in scrolling zombie-mode,
Shelly does the same.
I wish I had never bought her that silly thing.
Hoof technology is amazing
but everything I hear about social media, it's dangerous.
I use mine to keep in touch with friends,
and yes, I might watch the odd video here and there,
but if I dare take that phone off Shelly, there would be uproar.

She says her imagination will run wild,
out of control if she has nothing to do before sleep.
Her imagination is on pause,
she cannot use it properly because she has not given it the chance.
I don't want her to count on this device as her shoulder, you know?
But there is no arguing with her.
I am a bad mother if I argue my point.
Her point is the only thing that matters.

I need somebody to talk to her,
show her that I'm not some out-of-touch older ewe,
but her mother, with experience and a valid point of view.

I miss the simple days where we entertained ourselves,
where we went to bed with the lights off to save electricity,
but got used to being in the dark.
It did me good, it helped me grow.

Now growth only seems to matter on a screen with statistics.
Sheep were not designed to always be entertained,
being bored and occupying yourself is a positive thing.
Sheep's attention spans are dwindling,
as more and more is at their disposal.
I miss the olden days where we had fewer choices
but could actually choose and be happy.
Maybe social media is
the persuasive pill that leads your free will into mayhem.

With so many choices to persistently make,
how many choices will it take
for Shelly to choose
to break free again.

DISTRACTION PART 1

Are you listening?
Can you hear me?
You.
Yes, you,
the one reading.
Are you paying attention?
Are you overthinking about something which happened yesterday?
Or are you daydreaming about tomorrow or the near future?
Are you even present?
Or is time your nemesis?
Where you have no weapon against seconds,
destruction to your purpose,
destruction to your life construction is apparent.
You have talent, gifts,
yet you lack the discipline to respond to a challenge.

How many screens have you got going on?
While you read, are you also on your phone?
Doomscrolling.
Zoom calling.
Lost in technology that's meant to make us connect,
The word con is what stands out to me.
You are the sale,
if you buy into it.
It frustrates me as I see so much potential in you.

OLIVER

An enormous shadow
swallows sunlight.
Ginormous hooves,
skin ripped, toughened,
ribbed with callus,
claws, sharp.

Bass, low.
Oliver's voice vibrates the ground,
echoes through the halls,
ricochets back and forth
off of the nerve endings of other sheep.

Scorn, worn, menacing horns pierce the air,
curved with deep, ingrained, parallel patterns.

A chewer, a spitter, a starer,
a block of woven wool,
weaved into a tight, strong ball,
solid.

Dark eyes, scarred cheeks, thick skin.

Sheep move out of the way when they hear
the hoofsteps of Oliver's approach.
They tremble in fear,
eyes down,
engulfed.

'Oi you,
your mum's gonna die.
That's right, you,
your mum, your beloved mother is going to die
and it's going to be all your fault.

YOUR.
FAULT.
Loser.
Are those tears?
Poor you,
now drown,
before you get extremely ill.
You are awful, a disgusting, vile sheep,
you think the most sickening things.
You weak, waste of oxygen,
why are you still here?
Why have you not drank yourself into the deathbed yet?
I said drown.

...

'Well done. Look at the state you're in.
Don't you sulk. You ungrateful rat.
I really don't like the look of you.'

Oliver winds up his right front hoof,
'I'm going to beat you until you look like cooked meat.
You'll be haunted by the sound. Ever seen *Rocky*?
Where he pounds human thighs at the butchers.
I will butcher you, then feed you to Charles.'

'Your turn, Charles.'

CHARLES

Charles is less physically threatening,
with a quiet, calm voice.
Zero aggression.
But assertion.
With a hint of,
if you do not obey me then Oliver will take the lead again.
Sadistic.
Persuasive.
Misleading.
Manipulative.
Daring.
A ram with a plan.

'Oh, don't worry,
if you follow my lead and repeat,
then none of these things Oliver said will happen,
silly.

Now,
start to pray in your head,
repeat the prayer until there are no numbers left,
do it again.
Find a good number, the perfect number to end,
it must be perfect now.
Do not be interrupted or make a mistake,
otherwise you will have to start again,
from the very beginning.
Now, say the prayer in a different way for each point Oliver made,
ask to be forgiven for your sick thoughts, your bad thoughts,
repeat.
Ask for protection of your mother,
at least 30 times please.

Now you've done all of that, do it again,
and again.
Now leave your house,
go back inside your house.
Step on a specific wooden tile.
Do that exact process another 30 times.
Quick, run up the stairs and run down.
Do you feel run down?
Good, this means nothing bad will happen,
you are punishing yourself and it feels good, correct?
Repeat until you are exhausted.
Nothing left in the tank.
Get into bed,
get out of bed,
repeat.
Wake up.
Do not start something new,
not yet.
You must do as I say
before you start helping yourself,
please remember that.
Get in your car,
drive around the block, repeat.
You might have just killed somebody,
repeat.
Check you have not rammed anybody over,
repeat.
Get some new clothes on,
take the old off,
new on,
old off,
on, off, on, off,
keep going now,
you are on a roll,
light switch,
dodge that step,
walk in and out of the room.

Turn the TV on and off,
only use your forefinger.
Have a shower, get in and out, repeat.
Sit on and off the toilet seat.
Turn the tap on and off.
Hurt your skin,
pinch yourself,
punch yourself,
rip out your wool,
staple your finger,
repeat.'

DANIEL

'Oi you,
Oliver and Charles have told me all about you.
In my opinion,
you should be ashamed of yourself,
you have a bad attitude,
you really are a disappointing excuse for a ram.
Drunk and disorderly,
detrimental to your own mental state,
disorientated, drugged up,
disgusting thoughts,
you disgust me,
destructive behaviour,
they told me everything,
how sick you are,
how vile you are,
and how you blame them,
how you try to stop the natural order,
how you try to rearrange your mind,
you have no order,
no discipline,
no routine,
we must boss you around,
otherwise, who knows who you would be?
This is not your life,
it is mine: Daniel's.
You don't seem to understand.
Stop trying to resist.
I think you need another beating from Oliver.
We know you love disorder, really.'

JOURNAL ENTRY:
JOURNEY ACROSS THE SAHARA DESERT

We set off just the six of us,
on a trek of a lifetime.
Supposedly only 1% of sheep across Earth will ever visit the Sahara Desert,
as much as this is a challenge, it is a privilege.
We met the other twenty sheep from all over the UK who are
joining us on this journey,
through vast sand dunes and extreme heat,
they each have their stories,
their reasons why they had decided to take on this challenge.

It took us nearly ten hours to get into the desert,
our starting point,
an eight-hour bus journey followed by
the nearly two-hour jeep adventure was over!
There it is, the Sahara Desert.
I was baffled at how much the outskirts look like dried-up water,
a beach with no ocean, fossils everywhere!

We had so many giggles,
it felt like me and the rams were back in high school,
telling Dad jokes...

What do you call an ewe who loves the desert?
Sandy...

Terrible, I know!
But when we were in the moment, we were cracking up!
After all we were in the Sahahahahahahahara...
Alright, enough of that, I'll stop.

Trekking was tough,
the soft sand moved each hoof back half a step
as we tried to hike the terrain.

We finally reached the campsite,
where our tents were set up by extraordinary guides,
local rams, resilient and wise.
I chatted to some of them,
they told me about their families and how they miss them on these trips,
they told me how much they got paid,
it made me think about how fortunate I am —
they might never be able to ever afford to travel,
see another part of Earth.
The rate of their currency compared to pounds,
was shocking.

Food was awesome and everybody was on a high.
We were sleeping in the desert!
I loved watching shooting stars dance in the night sky,
away from all the light pollution that blocks out the beauty.

As we progressed further on the trek,
we began to get to know the other sheep,
they were all so lovely with interesting stories to tell,
our main guide from the UK an ex-service ewe,
now she was a real shooting star.
We were out there during Remembrance Day
and she read out a poem after a minute's silence.
The only noise we heard was the whistling of the wind.
Powerful.

The heat became an issue when it reached 37 degrees —
some sheep began to suffer,
I and a few others stayed back with those who needed help and
motivation
to keep powering through.
It was emotional, yet we saw the power of support and
encouragement.

We started to bond very quickly as a group,
every sheep supporting each other through the challenging dunes.

We set off at half five in the morning, to climb a seven hundred
metre dune,
then sat and watched the crisp sunrise,
something I've always wanted to see,
but the first time in the Sahara,
a special moment.
The soft sand filled my boots,
my wool made me extra hot,
but after thirty-eight miles over about two and a half days,
we completed the trek!

Our final evening saw us all together, laughing and having a drink,
I remember chatting with Lynn, one of the ewes on the trip,
she was missing her boys.
I got up and recited a poem I had been working on,
summing up our experience.
There were tears,
there were laughs,
it taught me the importance of sheep bonding and being together,
to support each other, through anything.
It made me think *What if the world did this?*
Imagine what we could achieve together
if we all focused on a common goal.

Will that ever happen?

Now that I'm home, I look back and realise how surreal the
experience was,
I chuckle when I find sand in my socks,
I am beyond grateful.
Wow, we did it.

NEWS REPORT: 'SNOW ANGELS'

Breaking news update on local lamb in desperate need of a liver
transplant:
a liver has become available.
The catch? It's a flight ride away,
with only 6 hours to get there before the donor liver in unusable.

The storm has been parading through this small town,
the deep snow making travel almost impossible.

As we wait to connect to our local reporter on the ground,
let's take a look into the journey of this poor young ewe so far.
The father of the young ewe has been working tirelessly
in order to pay medical bills.
The recently widowed husband of two
was in desperate measures to save his daughter's life.
Then, out of the blue, an Angel appeared,
a hairdresser who wanted to help —
she began raising money for the family,
raising awareness throughout this small town
of the serious condition of the young ewe.
Even going to the extent of finding a pilot and aircraft on call,
to take the father and daughter to hospital when a liver becomes
available.
But this storm is blowing time away...
Oh wait, we have a caller on the line,

'It's me, the woman you were talking about,
we are at the car park of the church in the centre of town
where a helicopter is landing to take them to the hospital.
I am calling on all sheep who are watching, nearby,
please, if you can lend us a hoof and clear the snow so the helicopter can land,
it would mean so much to this family,
please, we need you.'

You heard it here, folks, get down to the car park.
Bring your shovels, hats and gloves,
let's all work together for this young ewe and her father.

…

Our news reporter Anita Victor is at the scene.
Let's join her now:

Wow, hundreds of sheep have flocked together,
shovelling an enormous church car park for the helicopter to land.
The scene is beautiful,
sheep working as one for this little ewe and her father.
Wait, here's the truck.
The father and little ewe are here,
we are just waiting for the helicopter now.
I am getting reports the pilot cannot see the landing,
the reflection on the ground is too bright.
This cannot end this way.
This could be devastating,
moments away from a possible lifeline,
a life-changing moment for this family.

The sheep are taking off their coats and jackets,
laying them on the ground.
Genius! The pilot is lowering,
what a selfless act, as it is freezing out here.
Oh, these sheep are Snow Angels.

The father and daughter are in and are off!
The scenes are euphoric here in this small town,
everybody cheering, hugging, high hoofs all round!
Now that's what coming together,
the power of community spirit looks like.
An Angel really was watching over this flock this cold night.
I'm Anita Victor. Back to you in the studio.

JOURNAL ENTRY: INVINCIBLE

When a lamb is young, they are invincible —
I was invincible.
I could drink all night, then wake up and exercise.
In fact, I did.
I played a rugby match, had a drink with the rams,
then woke up and ran the Cardiff Half Marathon.
I was fitter back then,
no belly hanging low, to get in my way,
no breathlessness
I felt invincible.

It all caught up to me though,
the alcohol binges,
the poor choice in food,
I slowly began to feel less fit,
less
invincible.

Fatigue became my new normal,
I would wake up more tired than when I went to sleep,
I would be breathless when running,
I put on weight,
bags lived permanently under my eyes,
I felt low.

I began to think about my future, my old age.
If I kept up this lifestyle,
what would my seventies look like?
Would I even get there?

It took time but I decided,
to stop drinking,
to eat healthier,
to exercise more regularly,
to lose weight,
to feel energised.

I am preparing my body for older age.
When I get there,
I hope to still be fit,
to be able to work out,
to be strong, healthy,
with little to no physical issues.
I know what I do now
will impact what future me can do.
I am preparing for longevity.

As I began this journey,
I started to ask myself
why sheep keep thinking they are invincible.
Why have they not arrived at the same understanding as me?
I feel sad when I see people my age abuse their bodies,
I wonder what they are going through,.
I wonder if they know.
I hope one day they have the same realisation,
I hope they find peace.
I have listened to my elders,
taken their advice.
They are wise.

Now I wonder,
we get so caught up with life on Earth in tunnel vision,
some of us prepare for old age,
but not many of us see, the far, larger picture —
what we do on Earth affects us,
how we react, choices we make, words we use,
they affect our afterlife,
now my aim, is to prepare for this.
Old age will come and go,
but the afterlife
can be
eternal.

BAR

She said I'm not interesting...
because I'm not into resting...
You know, letting my wool down,
drinking,
experimenting,
investing in the escape,
the high she's obsessed with.

I told her
I put my interest in
my health,
I told her I'm into wrestling,
testing the limits of my body.
She was unimpressed with the fact that I eat meat.
She said,
'How can you be healthy, with dead animals rotting in your gut?'
I was taken back, she was all serious,
necking back the drink,
I thought I'd stay calm, I'm not one to judge,
and you know how long I've had a thing for her.
I disagreed with her choices,
but there's more to Barbara than a buzz...
I said,
'The meat I get is from the butchers, I eat organic, solely organic.
Low carb makes me feel alive!
Like I have energy running through my body all the time,
I feel stronger, have more focus and rarely get ill,
and even when I do, I don't use any pills,
I use food, food heals.'

She was like,
'Right...'
with a sarcastic sigh,
she kept sipping away.

I quickly said,
'I stand against animals being poorly treated,
living terrible lives in cages, frightened and weakened,
I stand for animals being treated with love and care,
living a healthy, happy life, one that is fair,
until the day that their time stops ticking, due to illness, injury or
old age,
I wish for them to be killed with grace, in a sheepane way.
Anyway, my diet is mainly meat and eggs.'

She rolled her eyes, shook her head,
and said,
'It's because of sheep like you, innocent humans are dead.'
She got up, stormed out, I was stunned.
I quickly followed, but she was gone.
I thought,
Oh forget this,
I dodged a bullet, but only just about missed it.
My stomach was rumbling
so I went home and cooked up some tasty beef brisket.

JOURNAL ENTRY:
THE LAST OF US

They say the world might end...

I just played this game,
where this ram and young ewe are in an apocalyptic warzone,
treading on bullet shells, every clip-clop forward, closer to death.
Randomly paired on a task to save sheepanity.

Years before, on the first day the world began to change,
the ram lost his daughter.
Something so tragic never leaves the mind.
It is caged until death.

The young ewe, vulnerable, courageous,
gave him a new purpose,
a second change to relive fatherhood.
They both connect and form human-like resilience.
The possible cure swims within her blood;
she was bitten by an infected sheep.
Those who are infected are violent, fearless, hungry, infested,
possessed by fungus that has zombified their minds and bodies.
It can get a bit jumpy, as they sprint at you
catch you off guard,
try to eat you alive,
as you scroll through what little weapons and ammo
you have to defend yourself.
You have to always be alert as you hear them follow,
I mean, who likes being stalked?
Some are blind yet advanced, sounds amplified,
the Bloaters are the worst, ginormous,
reload after reload, to bring them down,
it's like they are two sheep in one body,
freaky.

The game was awesome,
it made me think about the world ending.
Could it be a pandemic?
Could it be zombies?
Plants turning against us?
Or aliens invading?
What about a blackhole sucking us into its infinite vacuum of
nothingness?
There is so much talk
about how we could all be imminently destroyed,
not enough about what we could do
if we all came together,
a ginormous flock of sheep,
working towards the same goals,
imagine what we could accomplish,
imagine what we could achieve.
No more hungry stomachs, all mouths would feed.
Technology would probably see advancements beyond theories,
beyond philosophy,
astrology, geometry, biology,
cosmetology, our understanding of our physiology,
psychology, the oceans, the seas, marine biology,
neurology,
basically, any 'ology', would be go from impossible, to possibly.
Deep questions might be answered,
and utopia could be traded for our dystopian reality.

I sense the fear in our atmosphere of other sheep,
afraid of the end of the world as we know it,
but I have no fear,
I have faith,
I know how it all ends —
World War 3, AI, climate change, no,
even if that happens, though tragic it would be,
it would not be
the last of us.

DISTRACTION PART 2

Hey, you, are you listening?
Are you watching the news?
Are you trying to figure out who you are?
Are you stressed about finances?
Do you enjoy your job?
How will you make ends meet?
Even if money is not an issue, are you happy?

Society is the weapon against freedom,
the beast's weapon,

Distraction

by any means necessary,
to keep you further away from your purpose,
who you really are,
who you are meant to be,
using your gifts to uplift.

Distraction

to keep you away from your Shepherd,
your wise Shepherd,
who loves you.

Distraction

with the buzz of notifications,
you really are a sheep,
a lost sheep.
Remember,
The Shepherd watches his flock by night,
no lamb truly lost or out of sight,
you can get back on your path of purpose,
you know what is needed,
now put the phone down,
reunite with loved ones,
reunite with nature,
reunite with yourself,
reunite with your maker.

Begin as new,
reborn.

JOURNAL ENTRY: ABSENT

I am not there.
In conversation I nod,
I guess what to say in response,
you know, figures of speech,
observations of body language,
but I'm not there.
I want to be.
I yearn to be there.
I am desperately scraping my hooves, clawing against my mind,
to be there.

I see moments with her, amounting to nothing meaningful,
when she pours out her heart, I never say the right thing —
I would know what to say,
if only I was in the room,
I would know what to say,
but I'm not there.

My mind fixated on an irrational fear,
I must do my compulsion,
I must.

I don't want these bad thoughts to become visible,
so I disappear while
she laughs at TV programmes,
shows me videos on her phone.
I subtly smile,
pretend to be present,
moments of joy, of love, are at reach,
yet this terror interrupts, it feels indestructible.

My absence is beginning to strain our relationship.
What if we have lambs and their Dad is there... but not there?

My worst fear is to be an absent father.
I sense her tears,
her frustration, her sadness,
I want to hold her.

I will hold her.

FIRE

Burn the enemy with the tongue,
fire the enemy with the bullet of a gun,
burn the Earth, ashes to ashes, dust to dust,
burn the sheep, we will not discuss.

Throw the enemy like a discus.
Pull! Aim! Fire!
Throw in the grenades,
bomb, burn, incinerate, with rage.

How can society thrive with civil wars?
From arguing with neighbours next door,
to streets fighting streets,
cities against cities,
countries at war with countries,
the world at war, reasons undercover.
Will it take aliens to attack us for us all to come together?

Some sheep told me religion is the cause of all war,
but I disagree,
I believe it's greed,
a selfish want,
an evil need,
to be better than the neighbour next door.
But I question,
how many sheep will keep wanting more?
How many sheep will use religion as a vehicle for war?
A vehicle for selfish intent,
a vehicle to drive fear, to thrive on sin, pretend to repent,
to inflict ideologies with detrimental consequence.

Catastrophic sheep-made disaster,
all in the mind of terror.
As the reason behind religion
gets choked, the true written word hidden,
now non-religious sheep believe religion
to be a prison,
that faith is no escape,
that it is all fake and should be forbidden,
as it creates sheep demons that wear its mask,
for their own selfish reasons.

There are sheep out there who see through the poisonous gas,
who know the meaning of faith and see through evil's mask,
who follow the only Shepherd there is and ever will be,
they feel the presence of God and know the book is Holy,
live with a deep meaning of life, faith, be forgiving,
love thy sheep neighbour and refrain from sinning.

Some sheep say money is the root of all evil,
I disagree,
I believe it to be selfishness,
sheep happy to see other sheep suffer,
as long as they get what they want,
more money, more power.
But selfishness is in us all,
it begins small,
yet it can grow out of control if we let it,
as we worship ourselves,
satisfy our desires,
this only leads one way:
into the fire.

HOOF TECHNOLOGY 3: FUEL

Fuel, to get somewhere - fast.
We began with food,
sheep on four legs running in our past,
chasing deer to eat, so we could break the fast.
We walked over mountains, trekked through forests,
foraged fruit: berries, apples, oranges.
We were nomads,
we'd stay on the move,
sometimes we'd sprint away from foes,
to survive, stay safe, although,
we'd tiphoof quietly, nice and slow,
when out hunting rabbits,
aware of the dry, crunchy leaves,
it became habit,
using fuel for energy.

Until we moved to the bicycle,
a quicker way to travel,
zooming around on two wheels,
inventors' minds unravel.

Somehow, we took a leap,
into horseless carriages: the automobile.
We were very smart sheep.

The engineering of the engine,
diesel and petrol,
expensive,
huge pieces of metal.

Cars, motorbikes, planes, boats,
rockets, trains, trucks, buses on roads.
Travel made easy,
but could it get any easier?

Less expensive maybe,
or possibly a little cleaner?

The electric car appeared, along with the hybrid,
they were a hit with consumers, not a hit with the National Grid.
Far cleaner to run and less expensive on fuel?
Lithium batteries are made with petrol engines,
when they run out of power, they are not disposable,
they only pollute.

I once heard of a ram in the US who made the first engine that ran
on water;
when he refused to sell his patent, he was poisoned, he was
slaughtered.
They have the blueprints of his invention, but are missing key
parts to rebuild,
he hid them away in fear of the now, inevitable.

A car with the cleanest fuel,
although it wouldn't make oil companies money,
it broke all the rules,
it could travel just like the other cars,
get you from A to B,
water, the fuel that could reduce pollution,
save all that money,
water, what an eco-friendly solution,
the ram is dead, isn't that funny?

Make your own mind up,
but if we did have cars that ran on water,
do you think it would really wind up
the ones pulling the strings so much they'd send the inventors to
the slaughter?

JOURNAL ENTRY:
SORE HOOF EFFECT

The sore hoof effect:
when I have accomplished something,
other sheep praise me,
they raise my spirits,
thousands of comments bring my eyes to water,
I feel elated,
yet just one bad comment sends my mind into a spiral,
it gets to me, it affects me, it's like a parasite, viral,
it sticks out like a sore hoof among a million comments of praise.
Why did they say that? Do I write back? It's outrageous.
Many scenarios of back and forth run through my mind,
I question why I'm so affected, an answer I can't find.
Time heals, as after time I feel nothing from the hate,
from the negative, from the rude, from the keyboard warriors who
try to shame.

The sore hoof effect:
gets no light,
but the light will shine upon us when we die.
I believe our Shepherd walks with us through our lives,
outlining every choice, every second, every single moment of our
time.
Moments we loved, we laughed, we celebrated,
moments of joy, of happiness, of togetherness,
moments of suffering, of salvation, of understanding,
of overcoming, of perseverance, of knowledge,
moments of regret, remorse, sadness,
moments of anger, of destruction, of selfishness.
Moments.

The sore hoof effect:
I often think about death,
when I meet our Shepherd,
as He walks me through my life,
I worry I will become tethered,
to all the wrong, the mistakes I made,
those I didn't learn from or knew I was about to make,
whether it was for selfish reasons,
or the reason itself justified,
what I am trying to say is,
when it is my time,
I hope my life is not full of sore hooves,
that stick out, outweigh the good,
but the good outweighs the sore hooves, as it's in my best interest,
to live a life with a conscious effort to be sinless.

OCD

It takes immense mental strength to pick up the pen,
my thoughts are ink I splash on a page,
I think, I overthink, I splash, I flood.
My mind is heavy,
a deep, blue ocean,
the ink needs to bleed.

As I begin,
I write as though my mind's on a thin layer of ice,
or as though he's watching,
listening for me to be active so he can strike.
I skate the pen,
I check to see if the ink bleeds through,
it does,
heavily,
drowning would be too kind.

He is vicious,
a bully,
if I make too much noise, I fall victim to his torture,
his sadistic suggestions swim strong,
I cannot help but become magnetised.

He is frightening,
a monster,
with three heads,
who leaves me within a percentage of living,
he beats my mind, consumes my time, defeats my strength, feeds
on fear.
No days off,
but this is no job, no joke,
this is debilitating,
destructive, exhausting,
I am starting to break again.

Last time my mind was torn apart,
an ocean was released, a dark ocean,
I had this impulsive urge, this freeing feeling when I ran into the
road,
as a taxi was approaching,
perfect timing.
I wanted to hurt myself,
I wanted his noise to be silent.

I recently began thinking more and more about what he actually is,
it was not easy to write this,
he is a parasite,
swimming within every cell,
dropping miniature nuclear bombs onto every nucleus,
front crawling, scraping his way,
into every atom-sized gap,
a virus that is not detectable,
even writing the word *scrapes* he attacks,
he takes off the *s* and *c* and screams at me what is left,
repeatedly,
rapes...
as though he is violating every part of me.
I fear the parasite will reside in my mind until I die,
wriggling through every part of my sheep body to try and catch me
out,
if I get through one attack,
he is there with another,
far more frightening
than the previous intrusive thought,
yes, intrusive they are.
At least my pen is a little lighter now.

Have you guessed who it is yet?

BOMBSHELL

My dear,
tell me what troubles you?
I am here,
put your phone down,
talk to your nan.
I might have grey wool,
I know I'm old,
but these wrinkles tell a thousand stories,
many of them from when I was your age.
You can talk to me,
what's going on?

Nothing,
it's nothing.

Now then, we both know that there is no such thing as
no thing,
but if you're going to stay quiet,
perhaps you'll listen to an old ewe.
When I was younger we had no phones,
we had none of this social media business,
we had very little luxury,
but that, to us, meant we had everything.
Yes, times were tough,
we had to work, physically work,
we helped our parents harvest our garden,
grew our own crops,
potatoes, carrots, peas...
money was tight but we were alright.
I had my mother to talk to, she always knew what to say,
my father he worked hard, never spoke much,
but he made me feel safe.
We were happy.
My grandmother, she was my best friend –

I never knew my grandfather –
my grandmother always told me
I could be anything I wanted to be,
I believed her.
She said,
'If nothing is what you want,
nothing is not what you'll get,
for you will always get something,
nothing brings regret,
go outside, be more than you think you can be,
for you are everything you want and more
take the leap, you'll see.'

What does that mean?

It means, we are whoever we choose to be,
it means we have free will,
free will to come out of our shell,
or free will to stay in it.
What I am saying dear is that you are a powerful young ewe,
who is more than what you think you are,
and I want you to see the beauty in your reality today,
for when you get old like me,
sheep walk by, they do not care as much,
they do not listen, they take you for a fool.
They neglect my opinions,
they neglect me.
Us old sheep, we are invisible,
but you, my dear, are visible,
with the power to be heard.

Nothing you say will shock us,
your mum and I,
we are here for you.
Drop your bombshells on me, dear,
I promise I can help you.
I have picked up the pieces before,
when your grandfather was at war,
his mind was always adrift,
he eventually came back to me,
I was there,
now I am here for you, dear.
Talk to me,
I am here.
What ever is the matter?

JOURNAL ENTRY: GUIDE

It takes a journey through life,
the suffering, the hope, the loss, the love,
to recognise how blessed we are.

To be selfless and acknowledge,
life is not all about us,
when we gain this knowledge,
we can begin to help those who need us,
to be present,
we are weightless from worry.

The journey, an interesting one,
challenges, wins, failures, beginnings, learnings and an end,
the learning requires gratitude,
hope, self-reflection and courage,
with a grasp on, how to use intuition,
see opportunity, take risks,
see how society distracts us from deep thought.

Our lives have a plan,
we can leave it in His hands,
there is no need to search,
you already have what you search for most,
you just need to say the words,
our Shepherd will guide you.

JOURNAL ENTRY: GETAWAY

At last,
we are escaping the suffocating, polluted city.
The chains of the same monotonous modernity
are corroding slowly, by every metre.
The concrete, all that unnecessary concrete,
the engines, the screeches, the arguments, the speeches
of drunken sheep, stumbling, tripping over their four legs
on their way to a one-night stand's bed.

Breathe

I just got off the phone with Dad,
Mum is driving,
Shelly is reading, weirdly...
How can you read anything in the motion of a car?
My organs crash into each other just thinking of it...

It's getting dark,
I think we're close now.

I have taken up an old pastime of looking out the car window.
There is so much life out there in nature,
it gives me a sense of adventure,
green hedges and fields of grass,
fresh air – nothing better.
There's hardly any sheep around,
hardly any noise,
hardly any pressure,
just the usual internal voices.
The roads are windy, the lanes are narrow,
yet my mind is widened,
I see human beings out in the fields,

they look so peaceful,
together as a pack, as a family,
as though they have formed their own community.
I wonder what they say to each other.
How would they behave if they had our minds?

Sheep, well, we are mad.
There are of course some beautiful things
that happen with sheep when we get along,
when we get along...
But there seems to be so much wrong,
so much conflict,
it consumes our news,
our conversations.
There is so much beauty in sheep,
but why is it that all we talk about is the ugly?
The negative? The brutal?
Why are we not more like humans?

Wait... I have it, I have an idea.
Imagine.
This could be my next project.
I could finally write that book.
Critique our sheep society, in a unique way.
Shock the reader.
Be provocative,
impactful,
meaningful,
comical,
inspire change,
to make the readers realise how stupid we can be,
how brutal, how destructive we can be,
yet show the love that weaves in and out of the hate,
solder division,
by opening minds.
The title:
Imagine we Trade Bodies with Humans

ACKNOWLEDGEMENTS

I firstly want to thank God for all the blessings and opportunities presented to me, for all of the understanding of suffering He has given me. I thank you God for allowing me to persevere through my struggles with OCD specifically and living with type I diabetes as well as my negative coping mechanism: alcohol. This has not been easy,. However, through these struggles, I have learned so much and feel there has been beauty through my learning. I understand why I had to go through what I did and I would not ever change it. Suffering produces perseverance; perseverance, character; and character, hope' (Romans 5:3–4, my favourite verse in the Bible). I want to thank you, Jesus, for my beautiful, understanding, family, fiancé and close friends, as they have helped me tremendous amounts over the years managing these struggles. Thank you God for my creativity with an extreme determination and will to not let anything ever stop me from achieving. Finally and most importantly, thank you Jesus for giving me the ability to relate to others and offer them support with the power of words.

I love you, Mum you are my rock. I thank you for everything you have done for me in my life. Without you, this book would have not been possible. Thank you for always being there.

I love you, Dad. Thank you for your wise words of advice and for always being there. Again, this book would not have been possible without you. Thank you for everything.

To Evie, my beautiful fiancé thank you for putting up with me and all the late nights of writing! Thank you for your love and support always. I love you forever.

To my siblings and family, I thank you for all of your support. You mean everything to me. I love you. Special thank you to my brother Jake who is my biggest critic because he cares so much. Thank you, Jake, for your love and support. I always want to impress you with my work because I care so much about your opinion, thank you for always being there. Thank you, Grams for your encouragement! Thank you, Nan. I know you are above cheering me on love you.

To Christina Thatcher, thank you for showing me that a poem can have many poems within it. Thank you for believing in my work. Thank you for all of your patience with me as a student and thank you for the knowledge that you have shared with me during my MA in Creative Writing. Going from a Sports Coaching undergraduate to a Creative Writing MA was a bit of a difference, but you and Kate made it easy. Thank you for your guidance. I appreciate everything.

To Mak, my good friend and music producer thank you for your support throughout my journey. There is something else you are to me and that is a mentor. I appreciate everything.

To the Seashore Writers, thank you for allowing me into your secret, special group. You were there at the beginning of my professional writing journey. Thank you for all the encouragement and the laughs. See you at the Christmas Do!

Special thank you to Andy James and Andrew Howard for taking the time to read and offer feedback. Thank you to Dave Cannon, Taylor Edmonds, Dr Matt Morgan, clare e. potter, Vicki Ball, Anna Skeels, Trev Burgess, Hayley Buckley, Steve Brumwell, Tricia Harris, and my Creative Writing MA cohort.

To Jannat, thank you for approaching me and believing in my work when many others might have dismissed the way I write poetry, especially in spoken word form, then releasing it as a book. You saw what I was trying to do and went with it. We have definitely done something unique here! Thank you for your support and for everything.

ABOUT THE AUTHOR

DUKE AL is a spoken word poet, hip hop artist and creative practitioner living in Wales. Writing rhymes is his therapy. From a young age, he would scribble raps and poems in his old lyric book. It was his way of expressing himself; an escapism to challenge his OCD. A passion of words, flow and rhyme flared. After being diagnosed with Type 1 Diabetes at 23, the pen became even more vital, helping him process and articulate his emotions.

Now DUKE AL uses his craft to create impactful change, one rhyme at a time. *Imagine we Trade Bodies with Sheep* is his debut published collection.

His work has been featured by Go.Compare Six Nations Rugby 2025, FAW, Cardiff Rugby, Creative Cardiff, TNT Sports (Sport in Words for Black History Month on Sir Lewis Hamilton), FujiFilm UK, BBC Wales, Cardiff Metropolitan University, and BBC Scrum V for Six Nations 2022.

Follow him on Instagram and X: @dukealdurham